Read-About® Geography

Living Near the Sea

By Allan Fowler

Consultant
Linda Cornwell, Coordinator of School Quality
and Professional Improvement
Indiana State Teachers Association

ᏔᏢ Children's Press®
A Division of Grolier Publishing
New York   London   Hong Kong   Sydney
Danbury, Connecticut

Visit Children's Press® on the Internet at:
http://publishing.grolier.com

Designer: Herman Adler Design Group

Library of Congress Cataloging–in–Publication Data

Fowler, Allan.
    Living near the sea / by Allan Fowler; consultant, Linda Cornwell.
    p. cm. — (Rookie read-about geography)
    Includes index.
    Summary: Describes how people make their homes near the sea and how their lives are affected by the water.
    ISBN 0-516-21562-0 (lib. bdg.)   0-516-27053-2 (pbk.)
    1. Oceans Juvenile literature. 2. Human ecology Juvenile literature.
3. Marine ecology Juvenile literature. [1. Oceans. 2. Human geography.] I. Title. II. Series.
GF67.F68   2000   99-14942
                                        CIP

GROLIER
PUBLISHING

Do you live near the sea?
You may go there to have
fun swimming, playing,
fishing, or sailing.

These girls are building a sandcastle.

People who live near the sea don't always have fun. The sea can flood people's land and ruin their homes.

A house destroyed by the flooding sea.

A sea dam

In some places, people have solved these problems. They have built large dams to keep the sea away from their homes and land.

People who live near the sea often earn their living from the sea.

Some people catch fish for a living.

They ride in fishing boats that set out before sunrise each day.

A fishing boat

The port of Los Angeles, California

Boats set out to sea from a place on land called a port.

Some ports are small villages. Other ports are large cities.

Many people live near ports where cruise ships dock. Cruise ships carry people on vacation trips.

Some of the people sell things to vacationers from the cruise ships, or take them on tours.

Cruise ships in port

These workers are unloading a cargo of bananas.

Ocean freighters carry almost anything from bananas to automobiles.

Many people make their living by loading and unloading goods from the freighters.

In some places, people live near the sea in tall apartment buildings.

These apartment buildings are in Florida.

In other places, people live in small wooden houses.

These houses are on an island in the Pacific Ocean.

Some people don't just live close to the sea. They live right above it.

These homes have been built on wooden poles in the water.

People also live on top of rocky cliffs that rise above the sea.

These houses are in California.

People who live near the sea must pay careful attention to the weather.

Sometimes storms gather over the sea. They move toward land.

The wind and water can destroy buildings.

This storm has caused a flood.

A seawall in Galveston, Texas

Large ocean waves can wash the sand away from a beach.

So people build long seawalls that stretch out from the shore. These walls keep the waves from getting too big.

People who live near the sea like the salty smell of the air. They also like the sound of the waves crashing onto the beach.

Most of the earth is covered by water. There will always be people who live near the sea.

Words You Know

apartment buildings

cliff

cruise ship

dam

flood

freighter

port

seawall

storm

Index

About the Author

Allan Fowler is a freelance writer with a background in advertising. Born in New York, he now lives in Chicago and enjoys traveling.

Photo Credits

©: Liaison Agency Inc.: 5, 31 top left (Lee Celano), 9 (Alissa Crandall), cover (S. Dooley), 10, 31 center (Frank White), 25, 31 bottom right (Gary Williams); PhotoEdit: 28 (Myrleen Ferguson); Viesti Collection, Inc.: 6, 30 bottom right (Walter Bibikov), 22, 30 top right (Richard Cummins), 3 (Michael Javorka), 13, 18, 30 bottom left (Richard & Mary Magruder), 17, 30 top left (Richard Pasley), 14, 21, 26, 31 top right, 31 bottom left (Joe Viesti).